AN
UNOBTRUSIVE
VICE

POEMS

TONY ULLYATT

THE DRYAD PRESS LIVING POETS SERIES

People! Read Poetry

An Unobtrusive Vice

First edition, first printing, January 2018

Copyright © poems Tony Ullyatt, all rights reserved
First published in Cape Town, South Africa by
Dryad Press (Pty) Ltd, 2018
Postnet Suite 281, Private Bag X 16, Constantia, 7848, Cape Town, South Africa
www.dryadpress.co.za
business@dryadpress.co.za

Cover artwork and design and typography by Stephen Symons
Set in 9,5/14pt Palatino Linotype Regular
Printed and bound by Digital Action (Pty) Ltd

ISBN: 978-0-6399141-0-7

A harmless passion, surely,
an unobtrusive vice
this waiting game of making
small books of verse.

– Douglas Livingstone

How can I take an interest in my work
when I don't like it?

– Francis Bacon

I don't know whether I like it
but it is what I meant.

– Ralph Vaughan Williams

I needed my mistakes
in their order
to get me here.

W.S. Merwin

Contents

From the ashes

We need to be perpetually renewed, born again
from the ashes of a temporary state
of disintegration or death.
– David Cooper

1

winter was late anyway

I should have guessed
something had gone awry
in the seasons that long year
with birds singing
    so late
into the warm evenings

2

the colour of birds
clashes with the sun
late autumn leaves swirl
toward the darkness
clutching at my coat

3

rising sparsely into the cooling air
the smouldering shimmer of herbs
the crackle of fragrances colliding
with spice-sweet flames conceiving

the solitary bird

Like Icarus

Last night a brown beetle landed
on my desk. Not wanting it to die
in alien territory, I opened a window
and let it go. It made no attempt to fly,
falling eight floors to the pavement
as if it had no wings like Icarus.
I'm not sure which of us is more
stupid but the beetle made me
wonder what I thought I was doing
and momentarily who I had become.

The boy who would be Icarus

He learnt the story
from his father, a professor,
who knew more about mythology
than aeronautical engineering.
Missing only feathers and wax
he plunged like a clumsy swallow
from the top diving board.
It would have been nice
had the pool not been almost
drained at the time.

Recuperating
in the orthopaedic ward,
he understood the importance
of acquiring wings or growing
feathers. An exclusive diet of
bird seed and chicken food failed
to produce anything more
than massive amounts of gas
– but not enough to launch
a take-off or propel a flight.
He became a regular at orthopaedics.

The problem, he read somewhere,
was excessive bone density in humans.
He began drilling holes in his limbs,
sucking out the weighty marrow,
but the project stopped through
insufficient funding for painkillers.

Now confined to a special bed,
his arms and legs restrained
with the sort of straps needed
to attach wings for gliding,
he stares through barred windows
at an empty sky. Occasionally
a bird smashes into the window.
That makes him smile.

The unfallen birdman accounts for his success

when I fly like Icarus
the sun fails me

the supple wax never melts
the wings work

higher I rise and higher
toward heaven

the air always amiable
sympathetic

even though I scorch and burn
I never fall

only darkness compels me
to earth again

with my flesh ravaged
my soul remains

my solitary asset
I am appalled

no one tries to possess it
save it or heal it

then I hear it on the wind
louder and louder

the relentless malice of
a smoky laugh

haunting me until I fly
and burn again

Icarus reflects on his descent

Wherever the poetry of myth is interpreted
as biography, history, or science, it is killed.
– Joseph Campbell

1

The mythologies are quite flawed or inconsistent:
I'm supposed to have flown too near the sun.
The sun is supposed to have melted the wax
holding feathers and battens fast.
But mythology is a profligate fiction.

Science prefers a dispassionate discourse:

$$\frac{L}{D} = \frac{\Delta s}{\Delta h} = \frac{v_{\text{forward}}}{v_{\text{down}}}$$

That's the glide ratio: distance forward
over distance downwards for a glider flying
at a constant speed in still air. No hubris;
no imminent disaster in those words.

Although my speed was variable, the air
turbulent, the sun's warmth too feeble
to melt wax, still I was high enough to glide
safely into exile but for the glide ratio's
one perilous presumption: that the wings
won't fall off. But they did. And that was
my father's fault of course.

2

Mythologists rarely ponder how the cunning artificer,
the maker of the Knossos maze got it wrong.
He contrived wings for us to arrive alive, and *he* did.
My death owes nothing to defective wings or blazing sun.

The truth is I am victim of the gods' envy. History sees me
as my father's hubristic wayward miscreant, fittingly
drowned. What divine irony that you need to know
how to swim in order to fly.

3

Passengers on the passing ship witnessing the hapless
fall, agreed their journey had been most worthwhile.
Feathers washed up on the shore were sold as souvenirs.

Section II

Strangers at the altar

Looking at altars
through the light splintered
by sumptuous windows
I can almost see
that man on his cross.

Then the quietness
and the light offer
a momentary
elusive glimpse
into tranquillity.

There is something
in those shafts of light
that stops me seeing
enough to believe.

In every version
of that special face
I recognise someone
until I get close and
we find ourselves
strangers once again.

Sea Point, Cape Town

In the corners of the church
the dust of unanswered prayers
thickens in the exhaustion
that comes with the Mondays
after.

The ritual agonies of words, tears,
memories have staggered
through dark doorways into the light
of old candles and the mystical blue
smell of incense before making them
bleed.

Hunched on the pews like careless
piles of clothing, three old women
whisper, breathing in the light
and incense as they wait for the dust
to lift.

Haiku on the paper wrapper of a drinking straw

long thin paper strip / a single alternative / a one-line haiku

Senryu 1–6

the autopsy showed
an unfulfilled child living
in this dead adult

*

with a broken wing
the eagle is more helpless
than a hurt sparrow

*

we destroyed a tree
so we could build your study
pray for forgiveness

*

the sacrilege of
the wise child has always been
to search after truth

*

those who are born dead
find life difficult after
reality dawns

*

to have lived this life
is to watch the postman pass
with only a smile

The beautiful terrorism

even the saddest poem's a jest
writ on the ebb-tide's sand
– Douglas Livingstone

Victoria Bay, where the ebbing tide
allows pale lovers to scribble names and
draw quaint hearts with initials scratched inside
as well as matchstick couples on the sand,
their artlessness and youthful confidence
sweet testimony to their pure desire
wedded to an apparent permanence
to which such moments secretly aspire.
The incoming waves ignore their trespass,
swirling away those tattoos of love's brief
follies whose recollection might surpass
all prior hurt, their hopes waylaid by grief.
Those days, sublime seen through memory's prism,
fall easy prey to time's terrorism.

The vicious beatitudes of age: ten sonnets with a coda

You only love when you love in vain.
– Miroslav Holub

1

You are the rose amid my thorny days
whose perfume lingers through my desperate dreams;
your gentle budding near my fallow ways
swamps me like sudden rain in arid streams.
But at my age, there's a way of knowing
we shan't be lovers; for to continue
your heart's blind and quite delicate growing
you will need fine rains, not drought, within you.
Old gardeners take a sort of wise delight
in the beauty they can find to cherish
but still they know inevitable night
brings days when love and all things must perish.
Look in my eyes and you should see the cost
of knowing what I never had is lost.

2

Being you, of course you will have to leave:
love or good sense will demand it of you.
Being old, I know I'll be left to grieve
this last exquisite moment to love you.
We could have whispered wise words under stars
and shunned the music of the void's dark song
amid life's wrangle for the heart's last scars.
I have been time's laughing-stock all along,
but I do remember young love's glances,
the way its tremulous petals unfold,
the grace of its voluptuous dances
with their ripening passion always untold.
Your eyes anoint me to be one of those
who once knew love mightier than the rose.

3

Will I swamp my days with too many teas
slumped in the corner of some bleak café,
staring bewildered at the drying lees
embarrassed, knowing that I cannot pay
the price of my dreams? Or die indebted
to the vicious beatitudes of age?
Must I now confront all I've regretted:
the pain, the tears, the words, the loss, the rage?
The truth is I have no more love to give,
I fear I've talked most of my life away;
the water no longer flows through the sieve
and all that's left is desiccated clay.
As I start to unpack my winter clothes,
I catch a glimpse of my favourite rose.

4

Each day, knowing less than I should have known,
I become much more inappropriate.
With every season, fewer seeds are sown,
each year there's something less to celebrate.
A kind world would want us to be lovers
contrary to this bright indifference
where you are so very much another's,
where wisdom yields scant meaning and less sense.
In a world where little loveliness grows,
where such vast despair leaves us so forlorn,
let us grasp at the splendour of the rose
and learn the holy wisdom of the thorn.
Is it only in dreams we can belong?
Dreams may deceive us but are never wrong.

5

If there were dreams to buy, which would you choose?
Some have the wine-ripe taste of golden days,
others quite dull with bland insipid hues,
and more yet reek of vile chthonic ways.
In the brightest of them, we are lovers,
this gawky world defers to our behest.
Then the dreamer wakens and discovers
the overwhelming malice of the jest.
Birds etch the architecture of their needs
on the dawn's dark canvas; the last rose sways
beneath the weight of dew which no one heeds.
Dreams are stitched together with nameless days.
No matter for whom dreams were intended,
my dreams of you are so far from ended.

6

My perfect dream may find itself a place –
though not in the world where I am living –
because it needs a gentle sacred place
to enact its rituals of giving.
The truth is sad as perfect tenderness
made noxious by the rampant lusts of time.
It retains its potency, none the less,
a deadly antidote to the sublime.
There is no way I can make you love me
if you don't want to or would rather not,
so my dream may be unworthy of me:
a rose untended in a vacant lot.
If somehow we should ever meet again,
may circumstances be less brutal then.

7

Crouched among the last surviving pieces
of my life's wreck, I seek a chemistry,
some wizard's formula which releases
the wayward life from its grim history.
I remember how old trees looked in spring
wrapped, like roses, in brilliant splendour
and how love could seem an eternal thing
nourished in a world yet young and tender.
Now I confess that in the last resort,
I have learnt to share the alchemist's dread
that all life's elixirs in one retort,
may yield no lively gold but fatal lead.
Upon the remnants of this meagre pyre,
I must cremate the sweetness of desire.

8

When life decides to let my body be,
I shan't be missed by the constant seasons;
rivers will run to dryness or the sea
and hail will still smash roses for reasons
of its own. I have no fear dying
despite every chance I have squandered,
all the time and love I've spent in trying
to ponder what oughtn't to be pondered.
My unsought detours to reality's
other temples in regions still unblessed,
have left me tattooed with the heresies
that lead the unwise to unshriven rest.
When I come to die of whatever cause,
I want the face before me to be yours.

9

Will you save your next life only for me?
I've no reason to believe you'd choose to,
love knows nothing of the temporary:
death may be the only way to lose you.
Knowing that I've mislaid much tenderness
pursuing no way other than my own,
what right have I to ask you to redress
the fact that I deserve to be alone?
Love, like sadness, has no expiry date,
nor has the rose's perfume, though ignored;
I know this lesson's come to me too late
when I see how much passion I have poured
away. Though way may well lead on to way,
we know there is no next life anyway.

10

I have never learnt how to mourn love lost
and was never allowed to grieve or cry;
so despite all the lives my life has crossed
I still do not know how to say goodbye.
But there is a sense the time's approaching
when I'll need to learn what I'm meant to do –
for time's relentless scythe is encroaching
on the days I have left to be with you.
Our hearts should sing as birds do after rain,
nuanced like roses against sombre skies;
knowing we will not get this chance again,
dare we deny what we should realise?
If there's no way for me to love you so,
then teach me how to say goodbye and go.

coda

The individual's freedom of mind is fettered
by the ignominy of his financial dependence,

his freedom of action trembles
in the face of public opinion,

his moral superiority collapses
in a morass of inferior relationships,

and his desire to dominate ends
in a pitiful craving to be loved.

– C.G. Jung

Being Frank

in memoriam Frank Cameron, my maternal grandfather

1

He went to the First World War not much more
than a youth like the rest of them.
He returned a man, volcanic with the fury
of war erupting in his stone-deaf ears,
the upshot of a shrapnel wound
– or so the story goes.

His seven children were badly wounded too,
on the battlefield of his domestic rage.

2

Each morning, like a sacrament,
he dressed tidily, latched the wooden gate
of his dull and dowdy dwelling
then, relentless as a Mark I tank, rumbled
to the corner shop for twenty cigarettes:
Wills's Woodbines, State Express 555
or Player's Navy Cut. In his dour existence,
they were his daily ration of pleasure.

In the toilet at the top of the stairs,
an ashtray overflowed with butt-ends.

3

The corner shop closed years ago;
my grandfather and his children have all since died
in their own time and manner; his grandchildren
carry that wrath in their genes one way or another;
their injuries invisible but no less incapacitating than his.

I've never known who cleaned the ashtray.

My grandmother's oven door

in memoriam Frances Cameron, my maternal grandmother

My grandmother had an oven door
she kept on the tea-rose quilt of her bed;
she would point to it with hands
that fluttered like rare birds eager
to land and rest in some soft place.

From time to time, she would ask me
– then a child of only three or four –
to take the door back to the kitchen.
I couldn't see it; I lived well
beyond her delusional world,
but she would guide me to it
with her tremulous bird-hands.

Pretending to carry the oven door
to where it belonged, I thought she was
magic; she could see invisible things.

Now, I know otherwise: her terrible illness
was no illusion, just one of life's tricks,
taking her mind wandering gently
further and further away into that place
where her hands could be still as sleeping birds,
and the oven door hang on its hinges for good.

Two framed sepia photographs

in memoriam Hilda and Percy Ullyatt, my paternal grandparents

1

My grandmother –
unswayed by X-rays, blood tests, facts –
prodded and jabbed unconvinced fingers
into her healthy if somewhat flabby belly
for more than thirty years until rampant
malignancy eventually burgeoned.
She was glad; at last she could prove
to her own family and satisfaction
that she was as right as she had been
all along. She nodded her acceptance
of this wisdom from a swamp of clinical sheets.
Her prurient vision of a universe
fornicating pleasurably, enabled her
to hate her sex life and retire amiably
into the honeyed promises of a relentless faith.
She had hoped conception would remain
immaculate, frequently wishing her children
unborn to avoid the stigmata, the tangible
evidence of carnality. They survived.
With fifty-seven years and a substantial
measure of futility behind her,
she died of self-inflicted cancer.
Now her photograph stares from the sideboard,
her clenched face gilt-framed.

2

My grandfather
grew rhubarb with leaves as big
as umbrellas near the compost,
and huge brilliant roses that
perfumed summer evenings;
daisies in profusion poked
provocative faces through
his lawn's clipped precision
against his leathery will.
The best years of my life,
he'd say, *the very best!* referring
to the myriad times he enjoyed
after my grandmother's death.
In photographs of him, his broad open smile
betrays the angry knowledge of his eyes:
some other woman could easily have made
him a better wife. Still custom – or was it
friends? – tempered with a little malice
perhaps caused him to resort to having
GOODNIGHT SWEETHEART chiselled
into her granite headstone; he'd had enough
of her appropriate biblical quotations.
One day, smelling of tobacco and rhubarb
he rose out of his chair, whose embrace
he'd been able to relish much longer
than his devout and prickly wife's,
and died on his way to the carpeted floor.
He was eighty. From his photographs
it's impossible to tell if he discovered
ways to run toward wherever
his delicious pagan lusts had urged him.
Nothing but that smile, those eyes ...

Six responses to the death of my father

in memoriam Eric Ullyatt 1918–1991

1

My mother thought my father selfish
in no small measure, and careless too,
because he wrenched her from her kin
and traipsed her round the world for more
than forty years. Their itinerary would read:

1950: Nottingham	=> Calcutta
1953: Calcutta	=> Port Sudan
1956: Port Sudan	=> Nairobi
1963: Nairobi	=> Durban
1965: Durban	=> Mhlume
1966: Mhlume	=> Darnall
1967: Darnall	=> Chiredzi
1972: Chiredzi	=> Durban (again)
1985: Durban	=> Bloemfontein
1991: Bloemfontein	=> Wherever the dead go

2

Sudden death has something quite unseemly
about it, catching as it always does
both victim and survivors unprepared.

My father collapsed as he was about
to lower his pale and sagging buttocks
onto the toilet seat. His spectacles dropped
to the floor, unbroken, but somehow bloodied.

With his tracksuit pants around his ankles,
his penis nestled in its pubic bush
like a tiny fat cactus shrivelling
in some sad and vastly neglected place.

I tried to neaten him as best I could –
rigor mortis set in, his eyes betrayed
no more than they had done throughout his life.

3

The next day my mother gave me
his watch and some bits and pieces:

his oils and his brushes
though I cannot paint

his pencils and pastels
though I cannot draw

and his bloodstained glasses
though I cannot see what
they ought to mean to me.

4

And he had a passion
for trees I remember –

he never explained why.

5

I came to possess very few of his things:
two oil paintings (only one of trees);
some graceful pencil sketches; details
of the back garden at Number 8;
two pastels of Golden Gate;
and a photograph of him wrapped
in warm clothes joyful in his passion,
his hands and eyes busy in the act of making.
He was happiest alone with his talent.

6

And I have memories of him of course,
yet, he never said he loved me. Perhaps
he meant to one day. But still, that is
what I remember most about my father
when he died and I held him in my arms,
as I sat on the bathroom floor stroking
his hair and listening to his silence.

It's hard to tell

And did you get what
you wanted from life, even so?
– Raymond Carver

After a lifetime, my mother quite unwittingly
abandoned reality and drifted ever perplexed
into that same land of forgetfulness
her mother had emigrated to years before.
Cancer withered my mother to a bony wraith
with only one breast and a dead husband;
she remembered neither. Nor her only son.

She stood, staring out the window,
not knowing who I was or why I was leaving;
there was no wave, only the mask of a face –
no one behind the cadaverous eyes. I waved,
leaving her there motionless. She died soon after.
It's hard to tell if we ever missed each other.

Stan

Stan was my uncle. He wore a cap
and a muffler when he went to work.

He always whistled when he walked
to the bus stop or, later, riding
a bicycle when he could afford one.

He married my mother's sister;
she had these pretensions.
So she and Stan moved up the hill

to a better class of suburb
where no one walked to the bus
or, much less, rode a bicycle.

Stan had to buy a car and change
his name to Stanley; she insisted.

But still he whistled when he worked,
making their new house more congruent
with my aunt's preposterous affectations.

He whistled through all his pains
and joys and tribulations; but not so
loudly that the neighbours might hear.

Eventually, he stopped going to work;
then he stopped altering the house,
and then he seemed to stop altogether.

One cold foggy morning he woke up
to discover that he'd left his mind
in a peaceful dream he'd been having.

From then on, he sat in a deep chair
staring at the turning seasons
and never had reasons to whistle again.

Herbert

married my father's sister,
the girl with the hare lip.
He was the man who kissed her.
They lived their childless marriage
in their typical Scunthorpe house.

A small bird freed from stigma's cage,
she chirruped around his weather-beaten life.

Through the seasons he walked to work;
his steady trudge punctual and unhurried.
He never understood the rush of others:
Death's patient enough, he used to say,
it'll find them when the time's right.
He was not a garrulous man.

After work, he rode his cycle
to the allotment where he grew
vegetables and a few flowers just for her.

She died on the operating table,
most of Herbert died there too.
He never went to the allotment again.

He trudged his clockwork way
to work, shouldering his daily grief
until he went on pension. After that,
he sat staring out the front-room window
long after dark waiting for her.

At home he abandoned the upstairs rooms
one by one; their bedroom grew fusty,
the staircase laced tight by cobwebs.
His life seeped away in recollections
of her voice, her busyness.
At night he fell asleep in his chair.

The spaces of his life dwindled
until neither memory nor neighbours
could sustain him. They found him
still in his chair, staring, waiting, dead.

In the kitchen sink there was a cup,
a plate and a knife unwashed.

The government as biographer

my book of life like yours is
issued in the standard edition
no leather-bound collectors' item
too elitist and undemocratic

it is illustrated in a minimal way
one photograph somewhat out of date
I always choose to smile it makes me
seem amiable even happy
and the camera never lies

if you read my book of life
it will tell you things about me

        it will tell you my age
        but not my maturity

        it will tell you my height
        but not my stature

        it will tell you my birthplace
        but not where my home is

        it will tell you my nationality
        but not where my allegiance lies

        it will tell you I may drive a car
        but not if I can afford one

        it will tell you I may own five guns
        but not who I should aim at

my book of life provides facts
at least the state presumes that
under threat of dire penalties
I have provided facts even though
they scarcely begin to touch the truth

however these documents save us
facts prevent the truth being
invented in our name

Love's austere and lonely offices

One of the boys in our school dormitory
was the archetypal pain-in-the-arse:
you know the type – looking at their feet
whenever they have to venture down steps,
wearing a cotton vest summer and winter
to stave off chills threatening their life.

He ran away from school right after lunch
on one of those quite ordinary days.
He has never been found, although some
think he will return. I'd like to believe them
but the cynic in me wants to point out
the many subtle ways death can muster.

Still, to make certain the neighbours see
the implicit trust she has in her son,
his mother washes his vests every Monday,
just in case he should return and need one.

And as for women

I have always met them too early
or too late in their lives or mine;
a simple fact beyond the bounds
of coincidence or my own bad judgement.
Yet, if I have been unwilling to sing
and unhappy to lust in my usual way,
do not assume I have been loving
anyone any the less.

'Twixt and between

error
lies in the distance
between the eyes
and the desire

desire
lies in the distance
between the eyes
and the error

Some other time perhaps

1

At university, there was a girl I studied French with,
she didn't have a boyfriend.
I didn't have a girlfriend either, then.
After several weeks of classes, I asked her
if she'd like to have a cup of coffee.
She smiled graciously, and said,
Some other time perhaps.
Then she walked away.

From time to time, I would ask her
the same question: she always had classes,
essays or tests, something to do
that prevented us from spending half an hour
together in the student cafeteria, its plastic furniture
hardly the apotheosis of style or romance.
Eventually, I got the message: I stopped asking.

One day, I asked someone else the same question,
and she said, *Yes.*

2

Twenty years pass. I'm giving a talk to an audience
of school kids. After I've finished, a copper-haired girl
comes up and says her mother wants to meet me.
My brain asks, *Why?*
My mouth says, *Fine.*

A moment later, I face a stylish, affluent lady
edging towards or perhaps a little past forty.
I don't recognise her. She has to tell me;
she's my former classmate
two decades and three children later.

It's wonderful to see you again, she says.
My brain says, *Why?*
My mouth says, *This is a surprise!*

I smile the inane smile of the bewildered.
Over the years, I've often thought of you, she says.
I smile another inane smile; I'm still bewildered.
Strange as it may seem, she says, *I've missed you.*
My brain says, *Bullshit!*
My mouth says, *Really?*

*I should have had that cup of coffee
the first time you asked me*, she says.
She smiles a tentative smile.
We could have a cup of coffee now, she says.
I smile another kind of smile.
My brain says, *Why not?*
My mouth says, *Some other time perhaps.*
And then I walk away.

On the road from Harrismith

was the last time I saw you:
I was homeward bound,
you on your way
to a holiday perhaps.
In the eucalyptus's shade
your parked car was
a little worn, pale-blue
American right-hand drive;
not quite your style after
Roedean and Houghton.

By the roadside donga,
you were overseeing
two small girls taking
ungainly pees; I presumed
the man at the driver's door
was your husband. He looked
nothing like me. That made
sense. I recognised your walk,
the way you shepherded
the children into the car
– comfortable, domestic.

After twenty years, I still had
no doubt. I wanted to tell you
I could never have lived that
sort of life, not even for you –
so I drove on instead.

Triptych

We are betrayed by what is false within.
– George Meredith

1

Through your study window

white doves flap up to the gable
and squat like tangible blessings

all sort of birds strut and squabble
in daybreak's dew-damp light

hunger gives all aggression strength
scarlet clivias trumpet morning's urgency

slender lilies languish in consumptive
splendour beneath the willow's thongs

the thick succulence of green plants
grows tumescent in dappled shade

some might call the place idyllic
but they would never recognise

the many demons flourishing
amid this neat and apparent order

2

Against your study window

a large photograph of your son
nestles against a smaller of you two
your eyes typically just averted

in case the camera should catch you
revealing something you would not
choose to acknowledge or explain
on your desk a cheque from your ex-husband
I need some sort of metaphor
something beyond coincidence
to understand all that may lie
somewhere inherent in these things
an unpredicted alchemy
creates a portrait from still life

3
Outside your study window

I watch your old demons cavort
and ithyphallic flaunt themselves

incapable of nothing more
than prurient lust

still craving hot satisfaction
of their immediate desires and
indulgence for their nasty thrills

among the shadows I find myself
trying to learn acceptance

of living on the far-flung borders
of your grotesque labyrinthine world

Into the gaping maw: on moving house

Into the gaping maw of rubbish bags,
we dump the testimony of our lives:

> photographs of faces you no longer recall
> and some you do but prefer not to;
> a few scribbled lines twenty years old
> when you were in a different time and space;
> poems that never ripened,
> divorce agreements confirming you are legally
> incapable of human relationships and in some cases
> highly susceptible to matrimonial venom;
> eight-year-old bank statements reminding you
> you were always on a tight budget,
> not much has changed; more old photographs,
> some clippings of long-dead grandfathers, uncles,
> more distant relatives you never met;
> letters of an undying love that simply died.

With the rubbish bag's belly gorged, you crimp
that voracious mouth tight to ensure nothing escapes
waiting for the rumble of the refuse truck;
a gang of voices, an indifferent heave, a whistle,
and your past eases away noisily to be regurgitated
on a rubbish dump near the cemetery
to disintegrate with time, weather and the scavengers:
nothing worth recycling.

Bloemfontein Sunday blues: a satire

The feeling of Sunday is the same everywhere,
heavy, melancholy, standing still.
– Jean Rhys

EARLY MORNING

Woke up this morning just after dawn
the sun blazing on the horizon.
I had breakfast early, victimised
by a long night's insomnia. I realise
it's about 1 a.m. in New York
as if that matters
and about 6 p.m. in Auckland
as if that matters either.

Insinuating rain, some melancholy clouds
hunched over the hills, until a brisk breeze
bustled the grumbling thunderheads away;
another failed promise: clouds and people
so similar ...

I watered the desiccated lawn, patchy
as a chemotherapy patient's skull;
the plants perked up afterwards,
the grass too. In the process
I stood on a snail by mistake and killed it;
its slime-silver path drying to powder
where it had tried to make its urgent way
across the backyard's hot cobbles.
I felt guilty for a long while.

MID-AFTERNOON

I bought a Sunday paper, soon wishing I hadn't:

rapes, escapes, parliamentary japes,
divisions, revisions, misprisions, suspicions,
corruption, disruption,
strikers, bikers, brutalised hikers,
massive pollution, no solution,
fornication, copulation, ever-increasing population,
the greedy, the speedy, the needy galore
spiralling debts that no one regrets,
the lies and spies no one denies
all desperate to please the voracious Chinese,
secret discussions when speaking to Russians,
cruising, schmoozing, copious boozing,
drugs, bugs, hypocritical hugs,
hit men, shit men, utterly unfit men,
bores, whores, endless wars,
vanity, insanity, no one says it cannot be,
blue lights through lights, no one else has any rights,
the crack ou, the wacko, the profiteering frack ou,
playing lotto, getting blotto,
ducking, trucking, fucking whatever's to hand,
Woema, Zuma, another vicious rumour,
Amandla, Nkandla,
feckless, reckless.
A million woes, and so it goes ...

I made coffee, ate a rusk or two, caught
the drift of acrid braai wood firing up.

LATE AFTERNOON

Checked out the emails, nothing but spam
from Bongo Maggi; I've never met anyone
christened after a soup, except a Heinz.
Maggi wanted my bank PIN to load my account,
then the blessed Saint William wanted that number too
promising me an inconceivable amount,
shortly thereafter God himself offered me the same deal.

How strange! God, Saint William and Bongo Maggi
live at the same address and make identical
spelling mistakes; the new theology: Father, Son,
and Unholy Scam? Risking the brutal retributions
of Judgement Day, and the certainty of eternal
bankruptcy, I deleted their pleas. But still I wonder
why God's laptop doesn't have spellcheck.

EVENING

Now, it's lunchtime in New York
and almost Monday morning in Auckland.

And I'm here. Still.
As if that matters.

Next Sunday will be much the same I suspect
but
I'll take particular care not to tread on any snails.

Your olive-green raincoat: variations on a theme by Leonard Cohen

Your olive-green raincoat
can never be famous:
it's not even tattered or torn.

You bought it that summer
the rain was quite heavy;
since then, it's scarcely been worn.

And a man with a beard
peers into train windows
in search of his only true love.

He waits at the station
for every arrival;
her heart will fit his like a glove.

The widow is lonely
makes antimacassars;
her cats are fed fat out of tins.

There's a clock ticking loud
in a portrait-hung hall
but no one to laugh at her sins.

The man watching TV
craves someone to love him;
but his only friend is old age.

His sink's full of dishes
each one of them dirty;
your vase is full of dead sage.

And somewhere there's someone
who's playing the piano;
the music has been dead for a while.

She's singing a song of
an olive-green raincoat;
the words are so sad that I smile.

The dark night has fallen:
now everyone's singing
as stars peter out one by one.

And no one is bothered
about crucifixions
or just where your raincoat has gone.

Dragons and donkeys

for Douglas Livingstone after reading 'My Reckless Dragons'

I wish words were dragons I could battle heroically,
earning some lady's love or, better still, a silver token.
I wish peasants whispered my name with awe and reverence.
I wouldn't mind even a little fear, just an undertone
here and there, or perhaps a modicum of jealousy.
I should like my victories over strong rebellious words
recorded in the histories and maps of literature.
But there are no mythologies and legends in my struggle:
my words behave like donkeys, recalcitrant and stubborn,
self-willed and disobedient, they simply refuse to heed
the rope, the goad, the lash of craft or artifice, standing dumb
and unwilling to share the burdens I carry alone.

Annotations for a text by Breytenbach

en die gedig is die betekenis
van die gedig

1   the meaning the poet
has
can never be
the meaning the reader
has

2   poet and reader
may be one but never the same

3   the poem is a meeting-
place where compromise
compels each to delve
into the psyche's semantics

4   meaning does not rely
on concurrence
nor does the poem

5   the meaning the poet
invests
can never be
the meaning the reader
withdraws

6   meaning predicates paranoia
of the infinite

A peculiar faith in the word

for Michael Saville, my English teacher

Sir –
it's impossible to think
of addressing you any other way
although I'm sure it would embarrass you now –
anyway, Sir,
in those inhospitable wooden classrooms
(temporary structures from 1929 and still
in use) you spent term after term proffering
words like exquisite morsels
or clinical specimens, each seductive
with their own temptations.
You would try to show us their savour:
at first, the relish of a phrase;
later, the pleasures of a succulent line;
and eventually the subtle palates
of an entire poem. At other times,
we found a colder, cleaner delight
watching your scalpel-sharp mind dissect
a text to expose some gross malignancy
of craft or one of its minutest lesions.
You would demonstrate ways of telling the lie
from the genuine, diagnosing the small
rapid cancers of self-indulgence
that bring death to vigorous thought.
Beneath the harsh light of scrutiny,
each incision sought to celebrate
your peculiar faith in the word.

Years later, in a classroom erupting
with pimpled barbarians and hormonal
yahoos – in truth not very different from

what we had been, though I suspect none of us
would have been magnanimous enough
to recognise in those unkempt faces
any of our former selves – there I was, trying
to teach Magee's 'High Flight'; hardly any
of the class had been in a train or ship,
let alone an aeroplane. I did my best
to evoke the sheer sublimity of flying's
unfettered freedom, how barrelling through
blue sky one might almost know how angels felt.
But then, remembering you, and compelled
by honesty, I had to confess that I too had
put out my hand to touch the face of God
but, smiling graciously, He had turned away.

Sir –
with all due respect –
I ask what words
could you offer now that could
possibly fill my empty hands?

Towards a theory of translation

The head and the heart
speak different tongues;

they do not translate
easily, if at all.

Ars Poetica

Putting a comma in the wrong place can lead
to a sentence with completely different meaning.
– Anonymous

once
    I found myself living
    in a calm country
    with no one
               exiled
  by law
      compulsion
         or lack of love
once
in a desperate dream

*

once
    I found myself living
    in a calm country
    with no one,
               exiled
  by law
      compulsion
         or lack of love
once
in a desperate dream

Section VI

Picasso's *Don Quixote*

Round-shouldered in dejection,
straddling a shambling nag
with patient Sancho Panza by your side,
you still believe in the nobility
of your dreams and bear the frustrations
of reality with an indefatigable dignity.

Stupidity's only reward
is suffering:
    that is destiny
    and irony its means;
and though you may never prevail
persistently you will endure.

And so may it please you, my lord, to know
those who understand your plight
are profoundly moved by your fallibility.

Three Judith Mason paintings

1. *Leopard's Breath*

Here is the stark reality of death.
Marrowless and brilliantly clean
but implacable as the desert lands,
the skull, a masterpiece of symmetry
impossible for fallible human hands to make,
evincing its own special grace.

And out of the bleak and burning soil
the power of life erupts
        vigorous
                primaeval
daring to challenge
the epitome of its own dying.

There is a delicate symbolic struggle:
life prevails
and death is only a broken bone.

2. *War Memorial*

Emptied of hope, desire and love,
a perfect skull grimacing through
stone nurtures sombre blossoms
to cure the agonies of the flesh.
The miracle of hand and eye,
of craft and vision clutches
deep into the tombless fragments
of the holocaust we dare not forget
though a thousand years, a million

flowers may violate the rubble,
which hopes to hide the ignominy
of jackboot and fragile men.

3. *Judas*

I have often wondered
what you felt when
you had to visualise
a crucifix strung with flesh –
those silver pieces silent,
comfortable in your hand.

I suspect
with hindsight you would make
a different choice, but infamy
compelled you to hang
on some desolate tree.

A fly plants its corrupting kiss
on your unremarkable face.

A sort of wisdom: Lily Sandover Kngwarreye's *The Dreaming*

For those who have never known Earth's numinous mystery
as we do, we paint pictures of *The Dreaming*:

> the river's relentless blue curves its unspoiled way
> through riverine forests, a myriad trees and plants
> take on the pellucid moonlight its halo bright
> between the just-formed hills and outcrops' heave
> everywhere the ancestor spirits still journey.

This is the benediction of an unblemished world
that was always here until others came ...

It may yet return
if our ways of knowing and loving this Earth
become a sort of wisdom for them too.

The perfect geometry of instinct: on an ancient carving of a duck in flight

1

This time of year after their final gabble
about direction and the weather ahead,
they rise in the perfect geometry of instinct,
spiralling steadily over the lake
high beyond the trees toward the clouds
and the travail of their travels.

The lake surface quietens again
after the massive upsurge of turbulent wings –
the woods now empty of the last calls.

2

Then I did not understand how you could refuse
the mysteries of that necessary flight,
becoming an earth-bound sojourner instead,
the next few days and your anxious waddle
revealed the splintered wing bones.
What was I to understand from your brokenness?

That there is no easy passage
between the earth and sky,
perhaps some ancient theory
about the transmigration of souls
or something about the interconnectedness
of all things and the truth of Indra's net.

3

Later, with you healed and squatting on the veranda table,
the artist in me strove with a whittling knife and a modest sense
of colour to make you jubilant through the psyche's handiwork.
In your beady-eyed presence, my hands wrought you
in flight so you might begin that longer journey through time
to arrive safe and whole one day beside another lake.

The unknown road to somewhere:
on an anonymous painting found in a garage

One always wonders about roads not taken.
 – Warren Christopher

1

a mist-muffled road and a morning walk
that would have us believe they are
leading nowhere leaving us doubtful
risking the assumption we will know
when the mist clears

I keep walking
beneath the long vault of trees
a branch cracks and breaks somewhere
to the left with no apparent cause
a pine cone thuds on damp earth
wild boars grunt close by

2

I remember that white stallion
leaping out of grey air
a terrible surge of muscle and breath
loose in the forest baboons barked
at this invisible stranger then fell silent again

3

translucent light rouses my craggy celtic blood
as I walk the mist breathes through the forest
in the cold lake low in the valley the otters

4

I know this is the right road yet I'm suspicious
of the ferryman and wonder how long
the obol's acrid taste might linger on the tongue

5

there can be no going back
nothing will be the same
neither the place nor what we were
the fantasy of familiarity no more
than wish fulfilment tainted by nostalgia
a longing for the garden where children still play

Winter bird: on a painting by Shozo Ozaki

I'd rather learn from one bird how to sing
than teach ten thousand stars how not to dance
— e e cummings

Winter:
the earth draped
to the horizon
in that whiteness
that clenches
the eyes yet insists
you gaze upon it.
The filigree of
bare branches curves
with the deep snow
lodged there.
Amid a myriad shades
of glistening white
a small bird's silhouette
the epitome of stillness
in this starkest
of landscapes.
It knows this
is perfect weather
for carolling
its pure song resonating
far into the impeccable
quiet of the winter woods.
It's quite irrelevant
whether we listen.

'His lonely singularity': Michael Ayrton's *Minotaur* in The Arkville Maze

1

It's probably my pendulous scrotum you'll notice first,
then the aggressive stance, the right fist poised for the imminent
piston thrust of the arm, the horns honed to pierce a body through,
the breath's vulgar heat, the terror of my bloody reputation.

2

But my bovine bulk is as deceptive as Daedalus's pseudo-cow,
a necessary subterfuge to help me cope with the unspeakable
hurt of misrepresentation and my lonely singularity.
My deformity attracts attention everywhere,
the body's abominations monstrous stigma that cannot be
disguised in ways that mental aberrations and perversions can.

3

My birth made me a royal embarrassment, the public sniggered
at this unsightly hybrid child, Poseidon's savage joke.
None of this was my doing, yet I am the island's laughing-stock.
Eventually, Minos locked me into Daedalus's Labyrinth,
LABYRINTHUS: HIC HABITAT MINOTAURUS chiselled ineptly
on the wall, near its forbidding entrance. I have come to know
its every convolution. I have fathomed out the unfathomable.
Yet I remain Minotaurus, malformed and misconstrued, still
pining for a little sympathy or even love one day perhaps.

Section VII

Within the ambit of its quaint unfolding

this life has been so busy and so full
of missed things

a small life with just sufficient passion
to make pain
for those within the ambit of its quaint
unfolding

this life has been quite lacking those moments
of sweet grace
which sustain the divine illusion of
redemption

just a small life never able to share
with others
the dark terrors of its ecstasies and
loneliness

this life has been so busy and so full
of missed things
just a small unlovely life in its quaint
unfolding

Poetry is a piece of very private history
which unobtrusively lets us
into the secrets of a man's life.

– Henry David Thoreau

Poetry in its own way is ultimately mythology,
the telling of the stories of the soul
in its adventures on this earth.

– Stanley Kunitz

Acknowledgements

Thanks are due to the editors of the following journals in whose pages some of these poems first appeared, albeit earlier versions:

ARAS Connections (USA, online), *Carapace, Communiqué, Contrast, De Arte, imPrint, Literator, Mantis: Journal of the South African Association of Jungian Analysts, New Coin, New Contrast, Northern Perspective* (Australia), *Poet* (USA), *Sesame* and *UpStream*.

Some poems have also been included in books. Again, I have taken the opportunity of revising the texts:

'On Judith Mason's *Leopard's Breath*' in Frieda Harmsen's *Looking at South African Art*, (Cape Town: Struik, 1979, 30–31).

'Love's Austere and Lonely Offices' in *Soundings*, edited by Douglas Reid Skinner (Cape Town: Carrefour Press, 1989, 112); and in *A Writer in Stone*, edited by Graeme Friedman & Roy Blumenthal (Cape Town: David Philip, 1998, 28).

'A Peculiar Faith in the Word' in *The Lonely Art*, edited by Tony Ullyatt (Pretoria: Academica, 1993, 7).

The first part of 'Ars Poetica' first appeared as 'Poem with no title: 10' in *The Open Door Omnibus* (Cape Town: Buchu Books, 1993, 157).

'Your Olive-Green Raincoat: Variations on a Theme by Leonard Cohen' in *The Profusion of Choices Manual* (Pretoria: J.L. Van Schaik, 1997, 54–55).

'Sonnet 1' in *Carapace 100*, edited by Richard Goldkorn and Johann de Lange (Cape Town: Snailpress, 2014, 131).

Extracts from the poems of Douglas Livingstone, including the title, are reprinted with the generous permission of The National English Literary Museum and © The Estate of Douglas Livingstone.

Tony Ullyatt

Notes on epigraphs/quotations

Page 3

A harmless passion, surely,
an unobtrusive vice
this waiting game of making
small books of verse.

Douglas Livingstone, 'End of a World' in *A Rosary of Bone* (Cape Town: David Philip, 1975).

Page 4

How can I take an interest in my work
when I don't like it?

Francis Bacon, *ArtQuotes*, http://www.art-quotes.com

*

I don't know whether I like it
but it is what I meant.

Ralph Vaughan Williams quoted on the authority of Bernard Shore and Sir Adrian Boult in Michael Kennedy, *The Works of Ralph Vaughan Williams* (Oxford: Clarendon Press, 1964).

*

I needed my mistakes
in their order
to get me here.

W.S. Merwin, 'Wild Oats' in *The Moon Before Morning*, Copper Canyon Press, 2014.

Page 8

We need to be perpetually renewed, born again
from the ashes of a temporary state
of disintegration or death.

David Cooper, P*sychiatry and Anti-Psychiatry*, London: Tavistock Publications, 1967.

Page 14

Wherever the poetry of myth is interpreted
as biography, history, or science, it is killed.

Joseph Campbell, *The Hero with a Thousand Faces*, London: Fontana, 1993.

Page 22

> *even the saddest poem's a jest*
> *writ on the ebb-tide's sand*

Douglas Livingstone 'Libation to the Geoid, Station 23' in *A Littoral Zone*, Cape Town, Carrefour Press, 1991.

Page 24

> *You only love when you love in vain.*

Miroslav Holub ,'Ode to Joy' in *Selected Poems* Penguin, 1967, (Penguin Modern European Poets).

Page 29

The individual's freedom of mind is fettered
by the ignominy of his financial dependence,

his freedom of action trembles
in the face of public opinion,

his moral superiority collapses
in a morass of inferior relationships,

and his desire to dominate ends
in a pitiful craving to be loved.

C.G. Jung 'General Description of the Types' in *Collected Works*, 1971, Volume 6, para. 626.

Page 40

And did you get what / you wanted from life, even so?

Raymond Carver, 'Late Fragment' in *All of Us: The Collected Poems*, London: The Harvill Press, 1997.

Page 47

Love's Austere and Lonely Offices

The title is taken from the last line of Robert Hayden's poem, 'Those Winter Sundays' in *Collected Poems of Robert Hayden*, New York: Liveright Publishing Corporation, 1985.

Page 53

We are betrayed by what is false within.

George Meredith, *Modern Love*, (1862), stanza 43. The poem is a collection of fifty sixteen-line sonnets about the failure of his first marriage.

Page 56

The feeling of Sunday is the same everywhere,
heavy, melancholy, standing still.

Jean Rhys, *Voyage in the Dark*, London: Penguin, 2000 (Penguin Modern Classics).

Page 57

A million woes, and so it goes ...

The last four words in this line are taken from Kurt Vonnegut's *Slaughterhouse 5*, New York: Delacorte Press, 1969.

Page 63

En die gedig is die betekenis /van die gedig

The Afrikaans can be translated into English as:
and the poem is the meaning / of the poem.

Page 57

Putting a comma in the wrong place can lead
to a sentence with completely different meaning.

Anonymous on Wikipedia.
http://www.ef.com/english-resources/english-grammar/comma/

Page 76

One always wonders about roads not taken.

Warren Christopher in http://www.azquotes.com/author/2866-Warren_Christopher.

Page 78

I'd rather learn from one bird how to sing
than teach ten thousand stars how not to dance

e e cummings 'You shall above all things be glad and young' in *Complete Poems, Volume 2 1936–1962*, London: MacGibbon & Kee, 1968.

Page 79

'His lonely singularity' is Michael Ayrton's description of the Minotaur in his book, The *Testament of Daedalus*, London: Methuen, 1962.

Page 83

... for poetry is a piece of very private history which unobtrusively lets us into the secrets of a man's life.

Henry David Thoreau, Essay on 'Sir Walter Raleigh', Bibliophile Society, Boston, Mass. Printed exclusively for members of the Bibliophile Society, 1905.

Poetry in its own way is ultimately mythology
the telling of the stories of the soul
in its adventures on this earth.

Stanley Kunitz in an interview with Gregory Orr, March 15, 2012, https://www.youtube.com/watch?v=KGmzr1kGeoQ.

People! Read Poetry

OTHER WORKS IN THE DRYAD PRESS LIVING POETS SERIES

AVAILABLE NOW

A Private Audience, Beverly Rycroft
Metaphysical Balm, Michèle Betty

FORTHCOMING IN 2018

happier were the victims, Kambani Ramano
A short history of remembering, Stephen Symons

OTHER WORKS BY DRYAD PRESS (PTY) LTD

AVAILABLE NOW

Unearthed: A selection of the best poems of 2016,
edited by Joan Hambidge and Michèle Betty,

FORTHCOMING IN 2018

The Coroner's Wife: Poems in translation, Joan Hambidge

Available from good bookstores in South Africa and online at
www.dryadpress.co.za

Printed in the United States
By Bookmasters